Make Profits
from
Your Talents

By
Christy Tola

Library of Congress Control Number: 2013918942
ISBN: 978-972924043-0

Unless otherwise indicated all Scriptures Quotations are taken from the New King James Version of the Bible.

Part of the Proceeds Will Go Towards Talent Awareness Program for Youth & Unemployed Graduates.

Christy Tola Arts & Books
P O Box 4243
Oak Park
IL 60304. USA.

Table of Contents

IMPORTANT FIRST!

Is Your Soul Saved?

If you have not invited Jesus Christ as your Lord and Savior, this is the time to do so. This is because you need the help of the Holy Spirit. He is our Guide and Comforter in life. He can only come to you after you have invited Jesus Christ, and when you begin to Study the Scriptures, praise, and worship God. You also need Him to help you to make major decisions concerning your life.

"...If you confess with your mouth the Lord Jesus and believe in your heart that God has raised Him from the dead, you will be saved. For with the heart one believes unto righteousness, and with the mouth confession is made unto salvation" Romans 10:9-10.

Please say the Prayer below:

Dear Heavenly Father, I am sorry for my sins. Please forgive me. Jesus Christ, please come into my life and help me. In Your name I pray. Amen.

It is important that you follow these Instructions:

Prayer

Pray every morning and ask God to protect and order your steps throughout the day. Also, ask the Holy Spirit to reveal your Divine Purpose to you. As you do,

5

He will begin to order your steps and lead you to where you are supposed to be in life.

Read the Bible and Worship

It's important that you create time for your Daily Devotion with God. When you're about to start your Daily Devotion (twice daily is advised), saying the Scripture below will help you. Also, pray and ask the Holy Spirit to teach you, as you study:

"...He opened their understanding,
that they might comprehend the Scriptures" Luke 24:45.

As soon as you become a Christians, you are like a new born baby that requires milk. Likewise, our Souls require spiritual nourishments for it to develop. Therefore, reading the Bible and Praise and Worshipping God will provide the spiritual nourishments that your Soul requires. It will also protect you from 'spiritual infections', ease your pains if you are spiritually afflicted, as well as allow the Holy Spirit to come close and help you.

It's very important that you read the Bible every day but must be accompanied by Gospel Praise and Worship Music, or songs of adoration to God. This will draw the Holy Spirit to your situation quicker. I will advise you to incorporate reading the Book of Psalms during your Daily Devotion.

Reading the Bible generously will also help you to discern spiritual truth about your life and situations.

"I have more understanding than all my teachers,
For Your testimonies are my meditation.
I understand more than the ancients,
Because I keep Your precepts" Psalm 119:99-100.

As you study, get use to writing Scriptures on small/index cards to meditate on, memorize, and confess, during the day. This will help to protect your mind and strengthen you against temptations.

Go to Church and Fellowship
We are commanded to fellowship with other Christians. But it's important to ask the Holy Spirit to lead you to a Church.

"...Let us consider one another in order to stir up love and good works, not forsaking the assembling of ourselves together, as is the manner of some, but exhorting one another" Hebrews 10:24-25.

One of the major reasons for going to Church is because Corporate Anointing is sometimes required for certain breakthroughs and this is only possible in a church environment. You need the prayers of other Christians and the Pastor. (The Bible says, *One person will chase a thousand and two are capable of putting ten thousand to flight;* Deuteronomy 32:30).

7

Secondly, the Church is the Holy Spirit School and Classroom. This is where He teaches us, His Students. The Pastors/Ministers are His Mouthpiece. You need a good and experienced Pastor that has been trained by the Holy Spirit, especially if you perceive that you have a major mission to accomplish in life. God will use the Pastor of the Church to train you for your future Ministry or Divine Calling for your life. Therefore, it's important that you pray and ask the Holy Spirit to direct you to His choice of Church for you.

Baptism

Get baptized in your local church. Christians are commanded to do so in the Bible;

"...Let every one of you be baptized in the name of Jesus Christ for the remission of sins; and you shall receive the gift of the Holy Spirit" Acts 2:38.

Serve

As soon as you begin to attend your new Church, volunteer yourself as a worker in any of the Ministries. Also, pray for guidance to serve in the area of ministry that will be of great benefit to your future.

Ask for Guidance

It's also important to always ask the Holy Spirit to guide you in everything that you do, so that He can help you to prevent mistakes. You are permitting Him to help you if you ask. God is the Owner of our lives and the Earth that we live in. We will be operating in the dark if we do not pray or acknowledge Him in all our ways, we are likely to make some mistakes, which are preventable.

> *"The earth is the LORD's, and all its fullness,*
> *The world and those who dwell therein"*
> Psalm 24:1.

> *"In all your ways acknowledge Him,*
> *And He shall direct your paths"*
> Proverbs 3:6.

Love One Another

Love people as we are commanded and try your best to avoid malice and unforgiveness, so your prayers are not hindered. Use Isaiah 40:29 to pray for help if you're struggling in this area.

> *"A new commandment I give to you, that you love one*
> *another; as I have loved you, that you also love one*
> *another. By this all will know that you are My disciples, if*
> *you have love for one another"* John 13:34-35.

Please remember to share the Gospel with your relatives and friends.

God bless you.

Introduction

Every single one of us has God-given Talents that can make us to be financially independent.

"...To one he gave five talents, to another two, and to another one, to each according to his own ability..."
(Matthew 25:15).

We are not supposed to go through financial hardship in life, because our heavenly Father has placed in us blessings that are inexhaustible.

"There are diversities of gifts, but the same Spirit. There are differences of ministries, but the same Lord. And there are diversities of activities, but it is the same God who works all in all" (1 Corinthians 12:4-6).

Many people have valuable Talents which they are not using or are yet to be discovered. As the Scripture says, we must seek before we can find;

"Ask, and it will be given to you; seek, and you will find; knock, and it will be opened to you"
(Matthew 7:7).

If you have not discovered your Talents, this is the time for you to evaluate your life and take note of the things that you can do or create that can generate extra income for you.

The following Chapters are designed to provide useful Guides about how you can discover some of the Talents and Abilities that God has deposited into your life. So get ready for new developments and exploits!

My prayer is that your spiritual eyes will be opened, so you can see all the hidden blessings that you have, and may your life become better through your discoveries. In Jesus Name. Amen.

Christy Tola.

1

Different Kinds of Abilities and Talents

There are different kinds of abilities and talents that we all possess individually. These include running, jumping, swimming, cooking, drawing, singing and so on. In this chapter, we will be looking at various kinds of Talents.

"...To one he gave five talents, to another two, and to another one, to each according to his own ability..."
(Matthew 25:15).

When we look around us, we can see that some people can do some things better than others who are in the same field as they are. A very good example is a man called Huram in the Bible, whom King Solomon sent for during the construction of the Temple.

"Now King Solomon sent and brought Huram from Tyre. He was the son of a widow from the tribe of Naphtali, and his father was a man of Tyre, a bronze worker; he was filled with wisdom and understanding and skill in working

with all kinds of bronze work. So he came to King Solomon and did all his work" (1 Kings 7:13-14).

Huram was not the only one that can do what he was called to do, but because he was an expert in his field, he was called.

Let's briefly look at some of the most common Talents that are exhibited by people. As you do, think about where you might fit in, and which best describes your Abilities or Talents:

Talent for Making Things

Below are some examples of the above type of Talent that are exhibited by some people:

cooking
sewing
weaving
plaiting
barbing
song writing
singing, and so on.

Talent for Inventions

Some people have Talent for inventing things. Few examples of invented items are:

cars
aircrafts
insulated jackets
vacuum cleaners
thermos flasks
weight meter
toothbrushes
cellular phones, and so on.

Talent for Speaking in Public Places/Events

Some people can speak better than others when they are engaged in public events. Such Talent are exhibited by:

Motivational Speakers
Debaters
Preachers
Announcers
Radio/Television Broadcasters
Comedians, and so on.

Talent for Teaching

Some people can also do better than others in various teaching fields. Few examples are:

School Teachers
Lecturers

Tutorial Nurses
Soccer Coaches
Head Mechanics
Swimming Instructors
Bible Teachers
Sunday School Teachers etc.

Talent for Providing Services

Some people are endowed with wisdom to do things smartly than others, when they are providing specialized services. Some will become master at doing the job. Some examples can be found in the following areas:

plumbing
watch repairing
shoe repairing
flower arrangements, and so on.

Other Talents can be found in people who are in fields such as; the military, weather forecasting, and so on.

Workplace Blessings

Some Talents can be physically transferred if you work in some manufacturing companies. After some years, what you have learnt from working with them will become part of you. If the company is producing things that are of interests to you, you can develop the knowledge and skills that you have acquired from them, just in case you'll like to start a similar business of your own in future. There are hidden treasures in such knowledge.

Ask the Holy Spirit to open your eyes to see how you can benefit from what you have learnt, and to also give you divine ideas to be creative.

"Ask, and it will be given to you..." (Matthew 7:7).

(There are some blank pages for recording business opportunities from your current employer and any new divine ideas that you may have received at back of this booklet).

Overlooked Blessings

Some Talents can also be in other forms that are not mentioned above. They are blessings that we can easily overlook because they are in us. For example, any beautiful area of our body that can be used to generate money is a form of Talent. Some examples are models, identical twins, those with beautiful face or shapely legs, attractive fingers, toes, or nails, and so on.

16

Comparing Talents and Inventions

Talents

Some Talents need to be developed while others require regular practice. Whatever the case may be with you, you need to improve your skills so that you can become better at doing whatever God wants you to do in life. For example, Talents such as swimming, basketball, soccer, and so on, will require regular practice.

Inventions

In the case of Inventions, the ideas for the products are divinely imparted. Also, all invented products are required to be tried and tested several times before they are released to consumers.

As said earlier, if you have not discovered your Talent(s), you have to prayerfully evaluate yourself to find out what God has deposited in you.

Task: Make a list of some of the things that you enjoy doing or making that no one has taught you. Secondly, ask the Holy Spirit to guide you about the one that you should focus on at the moment, if you have more than one talent.

As soon as you begin to focus on your God-given Talent(s), God will give you divine wisdom to be more creative. Write down the ideas immediately you receive them and start to do something. Some people are multi-talented. Who knows, you could be one of them! Don't allow any of your God-given Talents to be wasted.

(There is a Talent Evaluation Worksheet designed to help you to identify your Talents towards the end of this Book).

This is important!
If you have not accepted Jesus Christ as your Lord and Savior, this is the time to do so. As you evaluate your Talents, you need the help of the Holy Spirit to guide you, so that you can make the right decision. He can only come to you, after you have accepted Jesus Christ.

"...If you confess with your mouth the Lord Jesus and believe in your heart that God has raised Him from the dead, you will be saved. For with the heart one believes unto righteousness, and with the mouth confession is made unto salvation" (Romans 10:9-10).

Please say the Prayer below:

Dear Heavenly Father, I am sorry for my sins. Please forgive me. Jesus Christ, please come into my life. Let the Holy Spirit come and help me and reveal my divine purpose to me. In Your Name I pray. Amen.

(There are more information for new Christians at the end of this Booklet).

2

Resources

"For which of you, intending to build a tower, does not sit down first and count the cost, whether he has enough to finish it" (Luke 14:28).

To get anything started, you need some materials to work with, and the necessary finance. These are your Resources. Some of your requirements may be equipment, tools, or training, that will help you to sharpen your skills. You will also need the help of some people. All the above listed resources and more, are required for the development of your Talent(s).

Equipment

Let's look at a specific example. If you have a Cooking Talent and you want to start selling baked items, you will need simple equipment such as; a small/medium sized oven, serving cutleries, trays and so on. I will suggest that you should look for a Refurbished Kitchen Equipment Store for affordable items. You can also find some simple tools in Re-sale Stores near you. Furthermore, there are many Equipment Rental Companies that are listed in Yellow Pages or similar advertising media. Look for those with moderate rental fees.

Also, there are some Charitable Organizations that can assist you with simple equipment that will enable you to start your own business. The Internet is the best place to search for organizations offering such services. You can also contact your local city office or your local library for a list of organizations that provide various assistances to new entrepreneurs.

Training

Talents such as athletics or basketball, require constant practice and a coach. If you must hire a Coach and you cannot afford the fees, find someone to sponsor you. Your local church might be the best place to look for people that can sponsor you. Speak to your Pastor about your plans and ask him to help you find someone that can sponsor you.

Also, visit your local Library for a list of organizations that offer scholarship for the kind of training that you may require. You can also find out about some recreation centers in your neighborhood that provide free training or assistance to students.

It may also interest you that some Charitable organizations organize Talent Development Workshops and provide information and list of Resource Centers for people requiring assistance, which may be for personal development or new business venture. The Internet is the best place to search for such places. You will also find useful information about available grants that can help to pay for some of your expenses.

(It's important to watch out for spam websites, especially those asking for money for their services).

Helpful People

Pray that God should send the right people that will help you to be successful with your plans, when you are ready to put your Talents to work.

(There are some Scriptures and Prayer Points at the end of this Book).

Always hang around people with like passion as yourself. This will serve as a source of encouragement to you.

"As iron sharpens iron,
So a man sharpens the countenance of his friend"
(Proverbs 27:17).

Also, read books about other people's success stories, and emulate role models who made it from scratch.

Inventors

There are many organizations that provide assistance to New Inventors, which will help them to produce their Proto-types, the initial sample of what the final product will look like. Prayerfully search the internet for some reliable companies that can help you to produce your proto-type with moderate fees.

Important! Please be careful not to part with cash unless there are legal papers to back the agreement between you and the company.

3

Finance

Without money it's almost impossible to begin anything. Assistance for financing a project can come from grants, gifts from relatives or friends, scholarships, private sponsorships, employment or loans.

"Ask, and it will be given to you; seek, and you will find; knock, and it will be opened to you"
(Matthew 7:7).

Grants

I will advise you to search on-line for Government or Private Grants that are available for your kind of project. You can also visit your Local Government Office for a list of available grants. Your local library is also a good source of information.

Scholarships or Sponsorships

Don't hesitate to look for people to assist you with either a scholarship or sponsorship for your work. You never know who God can use to help you. Even if you feel humiliated initially when you have to go to people to beg for their assistance and you're turned down, humble yourself and continue to ask for help. Remember that God gives grace to the humble:

> *"God resists the proud,*
> *But gives grace to the humble"*
> (James 4:6).

Also, if you are a student, don't hesitate to solicit the assistance of some affluent church members or relatives for scholarship or sponsorship.

Personal Finance

If you are working, set aside some amount of money every month and start to do something about developing your talents. The least you can do is to place a jar in a corner of your room and start to collect spare coins every time you return from the store. They do add up to enable you to purchase few things.

Tips for Those Seeking Employment

Find some companies producing handcrafted items such as children's small teddy bears online. Some of the companies hire people to assemble products at the comfort of their homes. Also, some of them sell the initial raw materials for assembling to the people that they've hired, or give them out for free.

Don't forget that you can acquire some knowledge from some of the companies and use the knowledge to develop your own personal business in future. I will suggest that you should jot down some of the knowledge that you will gain while assembling their products.

(**For New Beginners:** when searching for such companies online, the key word to use is *'items for assembling'*. Again, be careful about parting with cash, and be sure about the authenticity of the website that you will be visiting. Look for the 'https' key symbol).

4

Conclusion

As said earlier, God has placed in us blessings and inexhaustible Talents, but many people are yet to discover theirs. There are more to us than we know.

"And He has put in his heart the ability to teach, in him and Aholiab the son of Ahisamach, of the tribe of Dan. He has filled them with skill to do all manner of work of the engraver and the designer and the tapestry maker, in blue, purple, and scarlet thread, and fine linen, and of the weaver—those who do every work and those who design artistic works". Exodus 35:34-35.

If you have not discovered your God-given Talent(s), you should begin to pray that the Holy Spirit should reveal it or them to you. Also, He will give you divine ideas to be more productive as soon as you begin to develop them.

Make sure that your products are market-worthy, when you begin to develop your Talents.

"Then God saw everything that He had made, and indeed it was very good..." Genesis 1:31.

"She perceives that her merchandise is good..."
Proverbs 31:18.

It's also important to find out information about obtaining Copyrights for your products. This will protect your products from being pirated by people.

Furthermore, it's important that you obtain a Business Permit from your local authority especially if you are doing business from your house. Most permits are inexpensive. Try your best not to do illegal business as this will free your mind from worries. Cherish your peace.

Think about sowing some seed in your Church towards realizing your dreams. The story of Hannah will inspire you about making vows (1 Samuel Chapter 1). Also, the Parable of the Talents will inspire you to do something about what God has deposited into your life.

"For the kingdom of heaven is like a man traveling to a far country, who called his own servants and delivered his goods to them. And to one he gave five talents, to another two, and to another one, to each according to his own ability; and immediately he went on a journey. Then he who had received the five talents went and traded with them, and made another five talents. And likewise he who had received two gained two more also. But he who had received one went and dug in the ground, and hid his lord's money. After a long time the

lord of those servants came and settled accounts with them
Matthew 25:14-19.

(Read the rest of the 'Parable of the Talents' in Matthew Chapter 25).

We are all accountable for how we use what God has placed in our hands. My prayer for you is that you will make Profits from your Talents and glorify God with them. In Jesus name. Amen.

Prayers Points

Scriptures

"...He was filled with wisdom and understanding and skill in working with all kinds of bronze work"
1 Kings 7:14.

*"...Israel shall blossom and bud,
And fill the face of the world with fruit"* Isaiah 27:6.

"...Hezekiah prospered in all his works" 2 Chronicles 32:30.

"...You shall remember the LORD your God, for it is He who gives you power to get wealth..."
Deuteronomy 8:18.

"...If you diligently obey the voice of the LORD your God, to observe carefully all His commandments which I command you today, that the LORD your God will set you high above all nations of the earth. And all these blessings shall come upon you and overtake you, because you obey the voice of the LORD your God"
Deuteronomy 28:1-2.

"Blessed shall be the fruit of your body, the produce of your ground and the increase of your herds, the increase of your cattle and the offspring of your flocks"
Deuteronomy 28:4.

"Blessed shall be your basket and your kneading bowl"
Deuteronomy 28:5.

"The LORD will command the blessing on you in your storehouses and in all to which you set your hand, and He will bless you in the land which the LORD your God is giving you" Deuteronomy 28:8.

"The LORD will open to you His good treasure, the heavens, to give the rain to your land in its season, and to bless all the work of your hand" Deuteronomy 28:12.

"Then this Daniel distinguished himself above the governors and satraps, because an excellent spirit was in him…" Daniel 6:3.

"…His delight is in the law of the LORD,
And in His law he meditates day and night.
He shall be like a tree
Planted by the rivers of water,
That brings forth its fruit in its season,
Whose leaf also shall not wither;
And whatever he does shall prosper" Psalm 12-3.

"She seeks wool and flax,
And willingly works with her hands.
She is like the merchant ships,
She brings her food from afar" Proverbs 31:13-14.

"She considers a field and buys it;
From her profits she plants a vineyard.
She girds herself with strength,
And strengthens her arms" Proverbs 16-17.

"She perceives that her merchandise is good"
Proverbs 31:18.

"...Go, borrow vessels from everywhere, from all your
neighbors—empty vessels; do not gather just a few. And
when you have come in, you shall shut the door behind
you and your sons; then pour it into all those vessels,
and set aside the full ones" 2 Kings 4:3-4.

"Nothing is better for a man than that he should eat and
drink, and that his soul should enjoy good in his labor.
This also, I saw, was from the hand of God"
Ecclesiastes 2:24.

Prayers

Let my spiritual eyes be opened to see all that God has deposited into my life

Let me flow in divine wisdom

Let creative power be imparted to me

Let my well of creativity not dry up

Let me be divinely connected to the people that will help me to be successful with my God-given Talents and Visions

Let me be divinely linked and find favor with those who will help me to make progress in every area of my life

Let my Talents blossom and bud and fill the face of the world with fruit

Let money be provided for me for the development of my Talent(s)

Let the spirit of excellence like that of Daniel rest on me

Let my visions exceed my generation

Let generational curses be broken from my life and family

Let the spirit of poverty and lack be broken from my life and family

Let my spiritual eyes be opened to new inventions

Let me see the hidden blessing(s) in my current employment (if any)

Let me live long to enjoy the fruit of my labor.

Talent Evaluation Worksheet

Please say the prayer below before completing the form:

I thank You God for creating me for your divine purpose. Please open my spiritual eyes to identify my God-given Talent(s). Thank You for providing for all that I will need to see it to fruition. Let it be used for Your glory. In Jesus Name. Amen.

A. Itemize Your Talent(s):

Please write down what you enjoy creating or doing. For example, cooking, singing, drawing, running, basketball, and so on:

(a)_____

(b)_____

(c)_____

(d)_____

(e)_____

B. Re-arrange them in order of preference:

(a)_____

(b)_____

(c)_____

(d)_____

(e)_____

C. Resources:

List the equipment and/or training that you may require:

Equipment(s)

_____

_____

_____

Training(s)

_____

_____

D. Finance:

Find out the amount that will be required for purchasing the equipment(s) or for the training that you have listed above:

$_____

Present Your Findings:

Present your findings to God and start to pray about them.

Use Deuteronomy 28 Verses 5 and 8, and other relevant Scriptures to pray about your Project.

Seek for Help:

I will advise you to do the following:

a. Seek the assistance of a relative or friend who can loan or sponsor you. Pray and ask God to grant you favor in their sight.

Use the Scripture below to pray when you are going to seek for help;

"...Esther obtained favor in the sight of all who saw her" Esther 2:15.

b. Find someone in your community or local Church who can give you menial jobs, (for example, washing their cars or cleaning their yards in exchange for pocket money). Use the money earned to purchase bits and pieces to help you get started.

c. Continue to pray daily on the Talent(s) that you have decided to focus on, at the moment, and try your best to start something no matter how little.

It's my prayer that you will succeed in whatever area of your Talent or Abilities that you decide to focus on at the moment.

"...He who has begun a good work in you will complete it until the day of Jesus Christ" Philippians 1:6.

Tips for Hearing Clearly from God

1. Read five or more Chapters of the Book of Psalms.
2. Say the following Scriptures:

> *"In all your ways acknowledge Him,*
> *And He shall direct your paths"*
> Proverbs 3:6.

> *"I will instruct you and teach you in the way you*
> *should go; I will guide you with My eye"*
> Psalm 32:8.

> *"My soul, wait silently for God alone,*
> *For my expectation is from Him"* Psalm 62:5.

> *"Oh, send out Your light and Your truth!*
> *Let them lead me..."* Psalm 43:3.

3. Worship God with your favorite gospel music or sing some songs of adoration
4. Ask God your questions. You should try as much as possible to exercise your faith and have a heart of expectation to hear from Him.

I will suggest that you should always keep a notepad and pen with you, so you can write down the Instructions that you will receive from God. He can speak when you least expected and in any form that He chooses-dream, vision, intuition or verbal. He can also send someone to you. But it's important that you write the Instruction(s) immediately you receive them and do as you are instructed.

It's also important that you avoid over-eating, especially if it's close to your bedtime. Try your best to prevent flesh from interfering with your spiritual life.

May God bless the work of your hand, Amen.

Worksheet for New Opportunities

Please say the Prayer below:

Dear Holy Spirit, please open my eyes to see all the hidden opportunities in my current employment(s). In Jesus name. Amen.

Job(s)	Opportunities	Resources
Job(s)	Opportunities	Resources

Job(s)	Opportunities	Resources

Divine Ideas

(Write down any divine Idea(s) or the Instructions to carry them out, as soon as you receive them).

_____

_____

_____

_____

_____

_____

_____

_____

_____

_____

_____

_____

_____

_____

_____

_____

_____

_____

_____

Divine Ideas

Divine Ideas

_____
_____
_____
_____
_____
_____
_____
_____
_____
_____
_____
_____
_____
_____
_____
_____
_____
_____
_____
_____
_____
_____
_____
_____
_____
_____
_____
_____

Divine Ideas

Divine Ideas

Divine Ideas

Divine Ideas

Divine Ideas

_____

_____

_____

_____

_____

_____

_____

_____

_____

_____

_____

_____

_____

_____

_____

_____

_____

_____

_____

_____

_____

_____

_____

_____

_____

_____

_____

Contact Details:

Christy Tola Arts & Books
P O Box 4243
Oak Park
IL 60304. USA.

Email: contact@tolabooks.com

More information about Pastor Christy Tola @ christytolaministries.org.

Facebook: Facebook.com/Christytolaministries

Youtube: Christy Tola Ministries

Instagram: Christy Tola

Search for Christy Tola's Books @ www.amazon.com

The Paperback Edition of 'Get Cleansed and Fill Your Lamp With Oil' and other Books by Christy Tola are now available at Amazon.com and other leading Bookstores.

www.ingramcontent.com/pod-product-compliance
Lightning Source LLC
Chambersburg PA
CBHW071336200326
41520CB00013B/3001